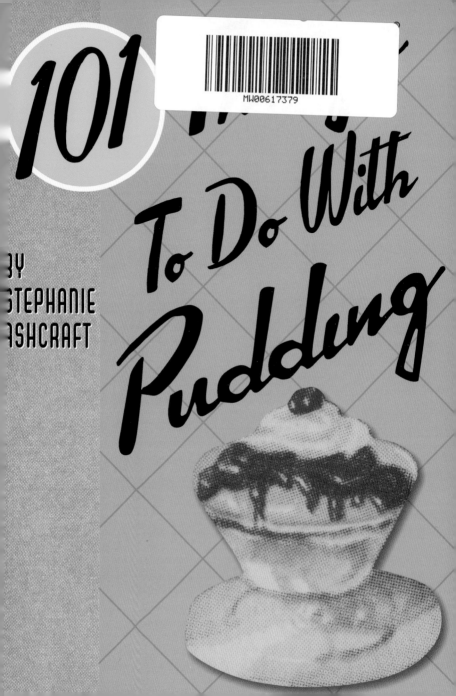

101

To Do With

Pudding

BY
STEPHANIE
ASHCRAFT

101 Things To Do With Pudding

101 Things To Do With Pudding

BY STEPHANIE ASHCRAFT

GIBBS SMITH
TO ENRICH AND INSPIRE HUMANKIND
Salt Lake City | Charleston | Santa Fe | Santa Barbara

First Edition
13 12 11 10 09   20 19 18 17 16 15 14 13 12 11 10 9 8 7 6 5 4 3 2 1

Published by
Gibbs Smith
P.O. Box 667
Layton, Utah 84041

1.800.835.4993 orders
www.gibbs-smith.com

Printed and bound in Korea
Gibbs Smith books are printed on either recycled, 100% post-
consumer waste, FSC-certified papers or on paper produced from
a 100% certified sustainable forest/controlled wood source.

Library of Congress Cataloging-in-Publication Data

Ashcraft, Stephanie.
  101 things to do with pudding / Stephanie Ashcraft. — 1st ed.
      p. cm.
  ISBN-13: 978-1-4236-0552-2
  ISBN-10: 1-4236-0552-7
  1. Puddings. 2. Quick and easy cookery. 3. Desserts. I. Title.
II. Title: One hundred and one things to do with pudding.
  TX773.A82 2009
  641.8'644—dc22
                        2009017192

I would like to dedicate this book to my two grandmas, Maybeth Dircks and Margery Woertz. They both passed their love of cooking down to me and I will be forever grateful. Grandma Dircks passed away in April 2009 at the age of 87 and Grandma Woertz passed away in May 2009 at the age of 91. I feel so blessed to have had so much time with both of these remarkable women. Our lives are truly shaped by those who come before us. I am thankful that I was born into such an amazing family. I have truly been blessed!

I would also like to thank Margie and Al Delgado for being our children's Marana grandparents! I don't know what we'd do without you!

CONTENTS

Helpful Hints 9

Pies & Pudding Squares

Cakes

Family Favorites

Dazzling Desserts

HELPFUL HINTS

1. Small boxes of sugar-free instant pudding can be used in place of the small boxes of regular instant pudding in most recipes. Low-fat or non-fat ingredients can be used in most recipes as well.

2. Vanilla, white chocolate, or cheesecake pudding mixes can be used interchangeably in most recipes.

3. Store recipe leftovers in the refrigerator. Most of the recipes in this book contain milk-based products and should be stored at a cold temperature before and after being served.

4. For best results, thaw frozen whipped topping in the refrigerator a day before you plan to use it.

5. For cakes, always grease and flour the cake pan, or spray it with nonstick cooking spray even when the cake recipe doesn't call for it.

6. Bake cakes and cookies on the middle oven rack, never on the top or bottom racks. To see if a cake is done, insert a toothpick into the center—if it comes out clean it's done. Or, if the cake springs back when touched, it's usually done.

7. For best results, use glass or stoneware baking dishes.

8. The first time you try a recipe, check for doneness 5 minutes before its minimum cooking time ends. Every oven heats differently.

9. For chewier and softer cookies and bars, take them out of the oven just as they begin to look golden and let them cool on or in the pan.

10. For recipes using gelatin, make sure the gelatin is completely dissolved in hot water before adding any cold water.

11. When using fresh fruit, dip it in pineapple, orange, or lemon juice to prevent it from changing color.

ROLLS, BREADS, & MUFFINS

CINNAMON ROLLS

4 cups	**bread flour**
¹/₂ small box	**instant vanilla pudding mix**
¹/₄ cup	**warm water**
¹/₄ cup	**butter or margarine,** melted
I cup	**warm milk**
I	**egg,** beaten
I tablespoon	**sugar**
¹/₂ teaspoon	**salt**
I envelope (.25 ounce)	**active dry yeast**
¹/₂ cup	**butter or margarine,** softened
I cup	**brown sugar**
3 teaspoons	**cinnamon**
I container (16 ounces)	**cream cheese frosting**

In a bowl, combine flour and dry pudding mix. In the pan for your bread machine, add water, melted butter, milk, egg, sugar, and salt. Spoon flour mixture evenly over top and then sprinkle yeast over flour layer. Set bread machine to dough cycle and start.

When the dough cycle finishes, roll dough into a 10 x 17-inch rectangle on a lightly floured large cutting board. In a microwave safe bowl, combine butter, brown sugar, and cinnamon. Microwave for 10–15 seconds. Stir and spread brown sugar mixture over dough. Starting with the widest end, roll dough into a log. Slice into 16 pieces and then place on a baking sheet prepared with nonstick spray. Allow dough to rise in a warm place for 45 minutes, or until double in size. Preheat oven to 350 degrees. Bake for 17–20 minutes. While warm, top with desired amount of cream cheese frosting. Makes 16 rolls.

ORANGE ROLLS

4 cups	**bread flour**
1/2 small box	**instant vanilla pudding mix**
1/4 cup	**warm water**
1/4 cup	**butter or margarine,** melted
I cup	**warm milk**
I	**egg,** beaten
I tablespoon	**sugar**
1/2 teaspoon	**salt**
I envelope (.25 ounce)	**active dry yeast**
I package (8 ounces)	**cream cheese,** softened
1/2 cup	**sugar**
1 1/2 tablespoons	**grated orange rind**
I cup	**powdered sugar**
2 tablespoons	**orange juice**

In a bowl, combine flour and dry pudding mix. In the pan for your bread machine, add water, butter, milk, egg, I tablespoon sugar, and salt. Spoon flour mixture evenly over top and then sprinkle yeast over flour layer. Set bread machine to dough cycle and start.

Preheat oven to 350 degrees.

When the dough cycle finishes, roll dough into a 10 x 17-inch rectangle on a lightly floured large cutting board. Mix cream cheese, 1/2 cup sugar, and orange rind together. Spread over rolled-out dough. Starting with the widest end, roll dough into a tight log. Cut into 16 pieces and place on a baking sheet prepared with nonstick spray. Allow dough to rise 25 minutes. Bake for 17–20 minutes.

Mix together the powdered sugar and orange juice until smooth. Spread over warm rolls. Makes 16 rolls.

OVERNIGHT PECAN STICKY BUNS

³/₄ cup	**pecan halves**
20 frozen	**Rhodes dinner rolls**
1 small box	**cook and serve or instant butterscotch pudding mix**
¹/₂ cup	**butter or margarine**
¹/₂ cup	**brown sugar**

The night before serving, layer pecans over bottom of a generously buttered 9 x 13-inch glass pan. Evenly space five rows of frozen rolls over pecans. Sprinkle dry pudding mix evenly over rolls.

In a saucepan, melt butter and then stir in brown sugar; bring to a boil, stirring constantly. Remove from heat and pour over frozen rolls. Cover with plastic wrap and leave sitting on the counter overnight.

In the morning, preheat oven to 350 degrees. Remove plastic wrap and bake for 20–25 minutes until golden brown. Invert on a serving platter so the "sticky" runs down the sides. Makes 20 buns.

CINNAMON PULL-APART RING

½ cup	**brown sugar**
1 small box	**cook and serve or instant butterscotch pudding mix**
¼ cup	**sugar**
2 teaspoons	**cinnamon**
20 frozen	**Rhodes dinner rolls**
½ cup	**butter or margarine,** melted

The night before serving, combine brown sugar and dry pudding mix. In a separate small bowl, combine sugar and cinnamon. Place one layer of 10 dinner rolls in a Bundt pan prepared with nonstick spray. Sprinkle half of brown sugar mix over the rolls and then drizzle with half of the butter. Sprinkle half of cinnamon sugar over top. Repeat layers with remaining ingredients. Cover with plastic wrap and leave on counter overnight.

In the morning, preheat oven to 350 degrees. Remove plastic wrap and bake 25–30 minutes. Let cool in the pan for 10 minutes before inverting onto a serving plate. Makes 10–12 servings.

BANANA BREAD

2 medium	**bananas,** mashed
$^{1}/_{4}$ cup	**applesauce**
$^{1}/_{4}$ cup	**vegetable oil**
$^{1}/_{2}$ cup	**water**
$^{3}/_{4}$ teaspoon	**cinnamon**
3	**eggs**
1	**banana or spice cake mix**
1 small box	**instant banana pudding mix**
1 $^{1}/_{4}$ cups	**finely chopped nuts or mini chocolate chips**

Preheat oven to 350 degrees.

In a large bowl, combine bananas, applesauce, oil, water, and cinnamon. Whisk in each egg, one at a time. Gradually stir in cake mix and then dry pudding mix. Fold nuts or chocolate chips into batter. Spread batter into two 9 x 5-inch bread pans prepared with nonstick spray. Bake for 35–45 minutes, or until a toothpick inserted in the center comes out clean. Makes 2 loaves.

CINNAMON BREAD

2	**eggs,** beaten
1 ½ cups	**milk**
¼ cup	**vegetable oil**
¾ cup	**applesauce**
1 teaspoon	**vanilla**
3 cups	**bread flour**
1 ½ cups	**sugar**
1 large box	**instant vanilla pudding mix**
1 ½ teaspoons	**baking powder**
½ teaspoon	**baking soda**
½ teaspoon	**salt**
2 teaspoons	**cinnamon**
2 tablespoons	**cinnamon sugar**

Preheat oven to 325 degrees.

In a large bowl, combine eggs, milk, oil, applesauce, and vanilla.

In a separate bowl, combine flour, sugar, dry pudding mix, baking powder, baking soda, salt, and cinnamon. Gradually stir flour mixture into milk mixture until smooth. Spread batter into two 9 x 5-inch bread pans prepared with nonstick spray. Sprinkle cinnamon sugar over top. Bake for 50–60 minutes, or until a toothpick inserted in the center comes out clean. Makes 2 loaves.

EASY LEMON POPPY SEED BREAD

4	**eggs**
1/4 cup	**vegetable oil**
1/4 cup	**applesauce**
1 cup	**water**
1	**lemon cake mix**
1 small box	**instant lemon pudding mix**
1/4 cup	**poppy seeds**

Preheat oven to 350 degrees.

In a large bowl, blend together eggs, oil, applesauce, and water with an electric mixer. Gradually stir in cake mix and then dry pudding mix. Stir in poppy seeds. Spread batter into two 8 x 4-inch bread pans prepared with nonstick spray. Bake for 35–45 minutes, or until a toothpick inserted in the center comes out clean. Makes 2 loaves.

PUMPKIN BREAD

5	**eggs,** beaten
³/₄ cup	**applesauce**
¹/₂ cup	**vegetable oil**
2 cups	**pumpkin puree**
I cup	**brown sugar**
I cup	**sugar**
2 cups	**bread flour**
2 small boxes	**instant coconut cream pudding mix***
I teaspoon	**baking soda**
I teaspoon	**salt**
I ¹/₂ teaspoons	**cinnamon**
I cup	**mini chocolate chips or chopped nuts**

Preheat oven to 325 degrees.

In a large bowl, combine eggs, applesauce, oil, pumpkin, and sugars until smooth.

In a separate bowl, combine flour, pudding mix, baking soda, salt, and cinnamon. Gradually stir flour mixture into wet mixture until just combined. Stir in chocolate chips or nuts. Spread batter into two 9 x 5-inch bread pans prepared with nonstick spray. Bake for I hour, or until the top springs back when touched. Makes 2 loaves.

*Instant vanilla pudding mix can be substituted.

BLACKBERRY MUFFINS

1	**white cake mix**
1 small box	**instant vanilla pudding mix**
³/₄ cup	**water**
3	**eggs,** beaten
¹/₂ cup	**applesauce**
1 ¹/₂ to 1 ³/₄ cups	**frozen blackberries,** thawed and drained

Preheat oven to 350 degrees. Prepare cups of muffin pan with nonstick spray and flour, or use paper liners.

Combine cake mix, dry pudding mix, water, eggs, and applesauce. Using a knife, cut blackberries into small chunks. Stir berries into batter. Fill muffin cups three-fourths full. Bake 19–23 minutes, or until light golden brown on top. Makes 24 muffins.

DOUBLE CHOCOLATE CHIP MUFFINS

3	**eggs,** beaten
¼ cup	**applesauce**
¼ cup	**vegetable oil**
¾ cup	**water**
½ teaspoon	**almond or vanilla flavoring**
1	**chocolate cake mix**
1 small box	**instant chocolate pudding mix**
¾ cup	**mini or regular chocolate chips,** frozen

Preheat oven to 350 degrees. Prepare cups of muffin pan with nonstick spray and flour, or use paper liners.

In a large bowl, combine eggs, applesauce, oil, water, and flavoring. Gradually mix in cake and pudding mixes until combined. Stir in frozen chocolate chips. Fill muffin cups three-fourths full. Bake for 25–30 minutes. Makes 20 muffins.

PECAN MUFFINS

I	**butter pecan or spice cake mix**
I small box	**instant coconut cream pudding mix**
4	**eggs**
½ cup	**applesauce**
I cup	**water**
I cup	**chopped pecans**

Preheat oven to 350 degrees. Prepare cups of muffin pan with nonstick spray and flour, or use paper liners.

In a large bowl, combine all ingredients until well blended. Fill muffin cups three-fourths full. Bake 19–23 minutes, or until light golden brown on top. Makes 24 muffins.

FRUIT SALADS

BERRY YOGURT PARFAIT SALAD

3 cups	**plain fat-free yogurt**
I small box	**instant sugar-free cheesecake or white chocolate pudding mix***
I bag (16 ounces)	**frozen berry medley,** divided
1/2 tablespoon	**sugar**
I teaspoon	**fresh lemon juice**
1/2 cup	**Grape-Nuts or granola,** optional

In a large bowl, beat yogurt and dry pudding mix 1–2 minutes with an electric mixer until well blended. Stir in 2 cups berries. Place in a 2-quart serving bowl or 8 x 8-inch dish. Refrigerate until ready to serve.

Thaw and mash remaining berries. Stir in sugar and lemon juice. Spoon berry mixture over salad. Garnish individual servings with Grape-Nuts or granola, if desired. Makes 4–6 servings.

*Regular pudding mix can be substituted.

GRANDMA'S RASPBERRY CREAM SALAD

1 small box	**raspberry gelatin**
1 small box	**cook and serve vanilla pudding mix**
3 tablespoons	**quick-cooking Kraft Minute Tapioca**
3 cups	**cold water**
1 cup	**frozen raspberries**
1 container (12 ounces)	**frozen whipped topping,** thawed and divided

In a saucepan, combine dry gelatin, pudding mix, and tapioca; add water. Bring to a boil, stirring constantly. Boil 2 minutes. Remove from heat and stir in frozen raspberries. Cool to room temperature. Transfer salad to a 2-quart glass bowl. Gently fold in whipped topping, reserving some to garnish top. Refrigerate until ready to serve. Makes 8–10 servings.

BANANA CREAM COOKIE SALAD

2 cups	**cold milk**
1 large box	**instant banana cream pudding mix**
1 container (12 ounces)	**frozen whipped topping,** thawed
2	**bananas,** sliced
2 cans (11 ounces each)	**mandarin oranges,** drained
2 cups	**miniature marshmallows**
1 package (11.5 ounces)	**fudge-striped shortbread cookies,** broken into small pieces
	shredded coconut

In a 3-quart glass serving bowl, beat together the milk and dry pudding mix. Allow pudding to set up for 2 minutes. Fold in whipped topping, bananas, and oranges. Cover and refrigerate. Right before serving, stir in marshmallows and cookie pieces. Garnish with coconut if desired. Makes 10–12 servings.

NOTE: Dip banana slices in lemon juice to prevent them from browning.

NUTTY GRAPE SALAD

I small box	**instant cheesecake pudding mix**
I ½ cups	**milk**
I pound	**green seedless grapes**
I pound	**red seedless grapes**
½ cup	**candied nuts***

In a large bowl, whisk together the dry pudding mix and milk. Fold grapes into pudding mixture, covering as many grapes as possible. Sprinkle candied nuts over top. Makes 8–10 servings.

*Grape-Nuts or granola can be substituted.

PISTACHIO PINEAPPLE SALAD

I can (8 ounces)	**crushed pineapple,** with juice
I small box	**instant pistachio pudding mix**
I cup	**cottage cheese**
I ½ cups	**miniature marshmallows**
½ cup	**chopped walnuts,** divided
I container (8 ounces)	**frozen whipped topping,** thawed and divided

In a I-quart bowl, combine pineapple and juice with dry pudding mix. Stir in cottage cheese, marshmallows, and walnuts, reserving 2 tablespoons nuts for garnish. Fold two-thirds of the whipped topping into pistachio mixture. Spread remaining whipped topping over salad. Sprinkle reserved walnuts over top. Makes 4–6 servings.

CHRISTMAS CRANBERRY LAYERED CREAM SALAD

I small box	**instant vanilla pudding mix**
I small box	**lemon gelatin**
2 cups	**water**
2 tablespoons	**lemon juice**
I small box	**cranberry or raspberry gelatin**
I cup	**boiling water**
I can (16 ounces)	**jellied cranberry sauce**
$1/2$ teaspoon	**nutmeg**
I container (8 ounces)	**frozen whipped topping,** thawed
	chopped pecans, optional

In a small saucepan, combine dry pudding mix, lemon gelatin, and water. Bring to a boil, stirring constantly. Remove from heat and stir in lemon juice. Chill at least I hour, or until partially set.

After placing pudding mixture in refrigerator, dissolve cranberry gelatin in boiling water in a separate bowl. Stir in cranberry sauce until well blended. Chill until partially set.

Gently stir nutmeg into whipped topping and then fold into cold pudding mixture. Pour into a decorative glass bowl or a 9 x 13-inch glass pan. Chill until firm. Spread cranberry mixture evenly over pudding layer. Chill for at least 5–6 hours before serving. Garnish with chopped pecans if desired. Makes 10–12 servings.

LAYERED FRUIT SALAD

I can (20 ounces)	**pineapple chunks,** with juice
I can (8 ounces)	**crushed pineapple,** with juice
³/₄ cup	**fat-free plain yogurt**
I small box	**instant French vanilla or cheesecake pudding mix***
2 cups	**fresh or frozen blueberries**
2 to 3	**bananas,** sliced
2 cups	**sliced fresh strawberries**
2	**peaches,** peeled and thinly sliced
2 cups	**seedless green or red grapes**

Reserve juice from pineapple chunks. Place pineapple in refrigerator until ready to use. Combine reserved juice, crushed pineapple with juice, yogurt, and dry pudding mix. Chill for 1–2 hours to allow flavors to blend.

In a 3-quart glass bowl, layer the pineapple chunks, blueberries (if frozen, thaw and drain first), bananas, strawberries, peaches, and grapes. Spoon pudding mixture over top. Makes 8–10 servings.

NOTE: Cut grapes in half if serving to young children.

*Sugar-free pudding can be substituted.

ORANGE CREAMSICLE BLUEBERRY FRUIT SALAD

I can (20 ounces)	**pineapple chunks,** with juice
I can (15 ounces)	**sliced peaches,** with juice
I small box	**instant vanilla pudding mix***
3 tablespoons	**Tang breakfast drink mix**
4 cups	**fresh or frozen blueberries**
I cup	**seedless green or red grapes,** halved
1½ cups	**sliced fresh strawberries**
2 to 3	**medium bananas,** sliced

Thoroughly drain pineapple and peaches, reserving all juice. Combine juices, dry pudding mix, and Tang. Refrigerate until pudding thickens.

In a large bowl, combine pineapple, peaches, blueberries (if frozen, thaw and drain first), grapes, strawberries, and bananas. Fold pudding mixture into fruit. Serve immediately. Makes 8–10 servings.

*Sugar-free pudding can be substituted.

LOW-FAT AUTUMN APPLE SALAD

1 cup	**cold fat-free milk**
1 small box	**instant sugar-free butterscotch pudding mix**
1 container (8 ounces)	**frozen fat-free whipped topping,** thawed and divided
3 1/2 cups	**unpeeled apple chunks**
1/2 cup	**chopped peanuts or pecans,** optional

In a 2-quart bowl, whisk together the milk and dry pudding mix for at least 1 minute until thick. Fold in half of the whipped topping and then fold in apple chunks. Spread remaining whipped topping over salad. Garnish with nuts, if desired. Cover and refrigerate until ready to serve. Makes 5–6 servings.

NOTE: Regular pudding, milk, or whipped topping can be used as well.

COOKIES AND CREAM PUDDING SALAD

2 small boxes	**instant vanilla pudding mix**
2 cups	**buttermilk**
1 container (16 ounces)	**frozen whipped topping,** thawed
2 cans (11 ounces each)	**mandarin oranges,** drained
24	**Oreo cookies,** chopped

In a large bowl, whisk together the dry pudding mix and buttermilk until smooth. Fold in whipped topping until well blended. Fold in oranges. Cover and chill until ready to serve. Just before serving, stir in chopped cookies. Makes 8–10 servings.

LEMON-LIME CREAM SALAD

2 small boxes **cook and serve lemon pudding mix**
1 large box **lime gelatin**
1 container (8 ounces) **frozen whipped topping,** thawed

In a 4-quart saucepan, make pudding following package directions. Remove pudding from heat.

In a bowl, make gelatin following package directions. Stir warm gelatin mixture into pan of warm pudding. Pour mixture in a 9 x 13-inch glass pan with tall sides. Refrigerate 4–5 hours or overnight. Just before serving, spread whipped topping over top. Makes 10–12 servings.

SALLY'S PUDDING SALAD

1 large box	**cook and serve lemon pudding mix**
1 small box	**cranberry gelatin**
1 small box	**raspberry gelatin**
1 container (8 ounces)	**frozen whipped topping,** thawed
	fresh raspberries, optional

In a 4-quart saucepan, make lemon pudding following the pie directions.

In separate bowls, make gelatins according to package directions. Stir warm gelatin mixtures into warm pudding. Pour into a 9 x 13-inch glass pan. Refrigerate 3 hours or overnight. Just before serving, spread whipped topping over top. Garnish with fresh raspberries, if desired. Makes 10–12 servings.

PUMPKIN GINGERSNAP COOKIE SALAD

35	**gingersnap cookies,** crushed and divided
I small box	**instant butterscotch pudding mix**
$^1/_2$ cup	**cold milk**
4 cups	**vanilla bean ice cream or frozen yogurt**
I cup	**canned pumpkin**
$^1/_4$ teaspoon	**pumpkin pie spice**

Place all but $^1/_4$ cup cookie crumbs over the bottom of a 9 x 13-inch glass pan.

In a 2-quart mixing bowl, beat together dry pudding mix and milk until smooth. Beat in ice cream, pumpkin, and pumpkin pie spice until well blended. Pour and spread pudding mixture evenly over crumb layer. Sprinkle remaining crumbs over top. Refrigerate before and after serving. Makes 10–12 servings.

NOTE: Sugar-free pudding and light or sugar-free ice cream or frozen yogurt can be substituted.

GRAHAM FAMILY'S SUNSHINE SALAD

Salad:

I large box	**cook and serve lemon pudding mix**
I small box	**orange gelatin**
2 cups	**hot water**

Topping:

I small box	**instant lemon pudding mix**
I cup	**milk**
I container (8 ounces)	**frozen whipped topping,** thawed
I can (II ounces)	**mandarin oranges,** drained

In a 4-quart saucepan, cook pudding according to package directions. Stir in dry gelatin and hot water. Combine well and pour into a 9 x 13-inch glass pan. Chill for 4–5 hours or overnight.

In a large bowl, whisk together the dry pudding mix and milk. Fold whipped topping into pudding until blended. Spread whipped topping mixture over salad. Lay orange segments evenly over top. Chill until ready to serve. Makes 10–12 servings.

COOKIES,
BROWNIES,
& BARS

NO-BAKE CHOCOLATE OATMEAL COOKIES

1 1/2 cups	**sugar**
1/2 cup	**butter or margarine**
3/4 cup	**evaporated milk**
1 small box	**instant devil's food pudding mix***
1/2 teaspoon	**vanilla**
3 1/2 cups	**quick oats**

In a 3-quart saucepan, combine sugar, butter, and milk; bring to a boil. Boil for 2 minutes, stirring occasionally. Stir in dry pudding mix and vanilla for 30 seconds. Add oatmeal, stirring until oatmeal is completely coated. Drop by spoonfuls onto a baking sheet lined with waxed paper. Let sit 15 minutes, or until set. Makes 24–26 cookies.

*Butterscotch pudding mix can be substituted.

SUGAR COOKIES

1 cup	**butter-flavored shortening**
2/3 cup	**sugar**
2	**eggs**
1 teaspoon	**vanilla or almond flavoring**
2 1/2 cups	**flour**
1/2 teaspoon	**baking powder**
1/2 teaspoon	**salt**
1 small box	**instant vanilla, cheesecake, or banana pudding mix**

Preheat oven to 350 degrees.

In a 2-quart bowl, beat together the shortening and sugar until smooth. Beat in eggs, one at a time. Stir in flavoring.

In a separate bowl, combine flour, baking powder, salt, and dry pudding mix. Slowly stir flour mixture into cream mixture. Refrigerate dough for 1 hour.

Using a teaspoon, drop balls of dough onto a baking sheet prepared with nonstick spray. Dip a glass cup bottom into a small bowl of sugar. Use the coated bottom of glass to flatten balls to a thickness of about 1/4-inch. Bake for 8–12 minutes, or until lightly golden around edges. Cool on pan for 3–5 minutes before transferring to a wire rack. Makes 30–32 cookies.

SOFT CHOCOLATE CHIP COOKIES

1 cup	**butter or margarine,** softened
3/4 cup	**brown sugar**
1/4 cup	**sugar**
1 small box	**instant French vanilla pudding mix**
2	**eggs**
1 teaspoon	**vanilla**
2 1/4 cups	**flour**
1 teaspoon	**baking soda**
1/4 teaspoon	**salt**
1 bag (12 ounces)	**chocolate chips**

Preheat oven to 350 degrees.

In a large bowl, combine butter and sugars until smooth. Stir in dry pudding mix, eggs, and vanilla.

In a separate bowl, combine flour, baking soda, and salt. Slowly stir flour mixture into pudding mixture. Stir in chocolate chips. Drop heaping teaspoonfuls of dough onto a baking sheet prepared with nonstick spray. Bake 10–12 minutes, or until lightly golden around the edges. Makes 36 cookies.

CHOCOLATE CHIP-SPICE OATMEAL COOKIES

1/2 cup	**sour cream**
1/2 cup	**vegetable oil**
1/4 cup	**water**
1 teaspoon	**vanilla**
1	**spice cake mix**
1 small box	**instant butterscotch pudding mix**
1 cup	**quick oats**
1 1/4 cups	**chocolate chips**

Preheat oven to 350 degrees.

In a 2-quart bowl, beat together the sour cream, oil, water, and vanilla.

In a separate bowl, combine cake mix, dry pudding mix, and oats. Stir cake mix mixture into sour cream mixture. Stir in chocolate chips. Using a teaspoon, drop balls of dough onto a baking sheet prepared with nonstick spray. Bake for 10–14 minutes. Allow to cool on pan for 5 minutes before moving to a wire rack. Makes 36 cookies.

CHOCOLATE PUDDING COOKIES

1/2 cup	**shortening**
1/2 cup	**butter or margarine,** softened
1/4 cup	**sugar**
3/4 cup	**brown sugar**
1 teaspoon	**vanilla or almond flavoring**
2	**eggs**
2 1/4 cups	**flour**
1 small box	**instant chocolate pudding mix**
1 teaspoon	**baking soda**
1/4 teaspoon	**salt**
1 1/2 cups	**white chocolate, mint, or peanut butter chips**

Preheat oven to 350 degrees.

In a large bowl, beat shortening, butter, and sugars until smooth. Beat in vanilla and eggs, one at a time.

In a separate bowl, combine flour, dry pudding mix, baking soda, and salt. Gradually mix flour mixture into creamed mixture. Stir in chips. Using a teaspoon, drop balls of dough onto a baking sheet prepared with nonstick spray. Bake for 10–12 minutes. Allow cookies to cool on baking sheet for 5 minutes before moving to a wire rack. Makes 32–36 cookies.

WHITE CHOCOLATE
COCONUT CREAM COOKIES

2 1/4 cups	**flour**
I teaspoon	**baking soda**
1/4 teaspoon	**salt**
I cup	**butter or margarine,** softened
1/4 cup	**sugar**
3/4 cup	**brown sugar**
I teaspoon	**vanilla**
I small box	**coconut cream instant pudding mix**
2	**eggs**
1 1/2 cups	**white chocolate chips**
3/4 cup	**chopped macadamia nuts,** optional

Preheat oven to 350 degrees.

In a medium bowl, combine flour, baking soda, and salt; set aside.

In a large bowl, combine butter, sugars, and vanilla; mix until smooth. Beat in dry pudding mix and eggs, one at a time. Gradually stir in flour mixture followed by chocolate chips and nuts. Drop heaping teaspoonfuls of dough onto a baking sheet prepared with nonstick spray. Bake 9–12 minutes, or until lightly golden around the edges. Makes 40–46 cookies.

PUMPKIN CHOCOLATE CHIP COOKIES

I cup	**buttered-flavored shortening**
I cup	**sugar**
I	**egg**
I teaspoon	**vanilla**
I cup	**canned pumpkin puree**
2 cups	**flour**
I teaspoon	**baking soda**
I teaspoon	**salt**
2 teaspoons	**cinnamon**
I small box	**instant butterscotch pudding mix**
I ½ cups	**mini chocolate chips**
I container (16 ounces)	**cream cheese frosting**

Preheat oven to 350 degrees.

In a large bowl, cream shortening and sugar and then mix in egg and vanilla. Beat in pumpkin.

In a separate bowl, combine flour, baking soda, salt, cinnamon, and dry pudding mix. Gradually stir flour mixture into pumpkin mixture until dough is formed. Stir in chocolate chips. Using a cookie scoop or a teaspoon, drop balls of dough 2 inches apart onto a baking sheet prepared with nonstick spray. Bake for 12–15 minutes, or until lightly golden around edges. Allow cookies to cool and frost with cream cheese frosting. Makes 36 cookies.

QUICK LEMON COOKIES

1 cup	**Bisquick**
1 small box	**instant lemon pudding mix**
1	**egg**
$1/4$ cup	**vegetable oil**
$1/2$ cup	**powdered sugar**

Preheat oven to 350 degrees.

In a 2-quart bowl, combine Bisquick and dry pudding mix. Add egg and oil and then stir until dough forms. Using a small cookie scoop or a teaspoon, drop balls of dough into powdered sugar and roll to coat. Place coated dough balls onto a baking sheet prepared with nonstick spray. Bake for 10 minutes, or until golden around the edges. Cool cookies on a wire rack. Sprinkle powdered sugar over tops, if desired. Makes 15 cookies.

PEANUT BUTTER
SANDWICH COOKIES

1 ½ cups	**milk**
½ cup	**creamy peanut butter**
1 small box	**instant vanilla or chocolate pudding mix**
1 bag (17.5 ounces)	**peanut butter cookie mix**

In a 2-quart bowl, whisk together milk and peanut butter. Whisk in dry pudding mix. Refrigerate until ready to use.

Bake cookies according to package directions; let cool. Place a scoop of pudding mixture between two cookies. Store in refrigerator. Makes 9–12 sandwich cookies.

YUMMY STRAWBERRY COOKIES

1	**strawberry cake mix**
1 small box	**instant cheesecake or vanilla pudding mix**
2	**eggs**
1 cup	**sour cream**
	powdered sugar

Preheat oven to 350 degrees.

In a 2-quart bowl, combine cake mix and dry pudding mix. Stir in eggs and sour cream until well blended. Drop stiff batter by small teaspoonfuls onto a baking sheet prepared with nonstick spray. Bake for 8–12 minutes. Cool on wire racks. Sprinkle powdered sugar over cooled cookies, if desired. Makes 40 cookies.

VARIATION: Lemon cake mix may be used instead of strawberry.

NOTE: Do not attempt to cook large cookies using this dough as they will not cook evenly.

BANANA NUT COOKIES

1/3 cup	**butter-flavored shortening**
1/3 cup	**butter or margarine,** softened
1	**medium banana,** mashed
2/3 cup	**sugar**
2	**eggs**
1 teaspoon	**vanilla extract**
2 1/2 cups	**flour**
1/2 teaspoon	**baking powder**
1/2 teaspoon	**salt**
1 small box	**instant banana pudding mix**
3/4 cup	**chopped nuts**

Preheat oven to 350 degrees.

In a 2-quart bowl, beat together the shortening, butter, banana, and sugar until smooth. Beat in eggs, one at a time, and stir in vanilla.

In a separate bowl, combine flour, baking powder, salt, and dry pudding mix. Slowly stir flour mixture into cream mixture. Stir in nuts. Using a teaspoon, drop balls of dough onto a baking sheet prepared with nonstick spray. Dip a glass cup bottom into a small bowl of sugar. Use the coated bottom of glass to flatten balls to a thickness of about 1/4-inch. Bake for 8–12 minutes, or until lightly golden around edges. Cool on pan for 3–5 minutes before transferring to a wire rack. Makes 34–36 cookies.

EASY GINGERBREAD
MEN COOKIES

I small box	**instant butterscotch pudding mix**
¹/₂ cup	**butter or margarine,** softened
¹/₂ cup	**brown sugar**
I	**egg**
I ¹/₂ cups	**flour**
I ¹/₂ teaspoons	**cinnamon**
I ¹/₂ teaspoons	**ground ginger**
¹/₂ teaspoon	**ground cloves**
¹/₂ teaspoon	**baking soda**

In a 2-quart bowl, combine dry pudding mix, butter, and brown sugar until creamy. Stir in egg.

In a separate bowl, combine flour, cinnamon, ginger, cloves, and baking soda. Slowly stir flour mixture into butter mixture until dough is formed. Cover and refrigerate dough for I hour.

Preheat oven to 350 degrees.

Roll out dough to about a ¹/₄ inch thickness on a lightly floured surface. Using a cookie cutter, cut out gingerbread men and evenly space them on a baking sheet prepared with nonstick spray. Bake for 10–12 minutes. Cool on a wire rack. Decorate each cookie if desired. Makes approximately 24 cookies.

CHOCOLATE CREAM-SMOTHERED BROWNIES

1 box (19.5 ounces)	**brownie mix**
1 ½ cups	**cold milk**
1 small box	**instant chocolate pudding mix**
1 package (8 ounces)	**cream cheese,** softened
1 ½ cups	**powdered sugar**
1 container (8 ounces)	**frozen whipped topping,** thawed and divided
½ cup	**chopped nuts or mini chocolate chips,** optional

Prepare brownies in a 9 x 13-inch pan according to package directions; cool completely.

In a medium bowl, beat together the milk and dry pudding mix for 1–2 minutes; chill for 5 minutes. Spread pudding over brownies.

In a separate bowl, beat together the cream cheese and powdered sugar until smooth. Fold in whipped topping until well blended. Spread cream cheese mixture over pudding layer. Sprinkle with nuts or mini chocolate chips, if desired. Refrigerate 1 hour before serving. Makes 10–12 servings.

M&M BROWNIES

I small box	**instant chocolate pudding mix**
2 cups	**cold milk**
I	**chocolate cake mix**
³/₄ cup	**chocolate chips**
I cup	**mini M&Ms**

Preheat oven to 350 degrees.

In a large bowl, whisk together the dry pudding mix and milk according to package directions. Refrigerate for 5 minutes. Stir cake mix into the pudding mixture until blended. Add chocolate chips. Spread batter onto a baking sheet with sides that has been prepared with nonstick spray. Sprinkle M&Ms evenly over top. Bake for 30–35 minutes. Makes 24 brownies.

NOTE: Mini Reese's Pieces or regular M&Ms can be used in place of mini M&Ms. If using peanut butter candies, use peanut butter chips instead of chocolate chips.

WHITE CHOCOLATE LEMON BLONDIES

I small box	**instant lemon pudding mix**
2 cups	**milk**
I	**lemon cake mix**
I ⅔ cups	**white chocolate chips**
I container (16 ounces)	**lemon frosting**

Preheat oven to 350 degrees.

In a large bowl, whisk together the dry pudding mix and milk according to package directions. Refrigerate for 5 minutes. Stir cake mix into the pudding mixture until blended. Add chocolate chips. Spread batter onto a baking sheet with sides that has been prepared with nonstick spray. Bake for 30–35 minutes. Spread frosting over top. Makes 24 blondies.

VARIATION: A glaze can be made to replace the frosting by combining powdered sugar with a little water and a little lemon juice until desired consistency is reached.

PUDDING-SMOTHERED BROWNIES

1 box (19.5 ounces)	**brownie mix**
1 small box instant	**cheesecake or chocolate pudding mix**
1 ½ cups	**cold milk**

Prepare brownies in a 9 x 13-inch pan according to package directions. When done baking, immediately poke holes at 1-inch intervals with the handle of a wooden spoon.

In a separate bowl, stir together the dry pudding mix and milk for 2 minutes with a wire whisk. Pour half the pudding mixture over warm brownies. Let the remaining pudding chill for 5–10 minutes. Frost the bars with the remaining pudding. Refrigerate at least 1 hour before cutting and serving. Makes 10–12 brownies.

PIES &
PUDDING
SQUARES

BERRY PIE

1 small box	**raspberry, strawberry, or other berry gelatin**
3/4 cup	**boiling water**
1/2 cup	**ice cubes**
1 small box	**instant cheesecake or vanilla pudding mix**
1 cup	**cold milk**
1 to 1 1/4 cups	**raspberries, strawberries, or other berries**
1 container (12 ounces)	**frozen whipped topping,** thawed and divided
2 (9-inch)	**pie crusts,** prebaked

Dissolve gelatin in boiling water. Stir in ice cubes until melted. Chill until needed.

In a separate bowl, beat together the dry pudding mix and milk until smooth. Whisk gelatin mixture into pudding mixture until blended well. Fold in berries and one-third of the whipped topping. Spread evenly between cooled pie crusts. Chill for 3–4 hours in the refrigerator. Before serving, spread remaining whipped topping evenly over top. Garnish with extra berries if desired. Makes 16 servings.

NOTE: If using strawberries, hull and slice before adding to the pie.

FESTIVE EGGNOG PIE

1 ½ cups	**eggnog**
1 large box	**cook and serve vanilla pudding mix**
¼ teaspoon	**pumpkin pie spice**
2 teaspoons	**vanilla**
1 ½ cups	**heavy cream**
1 (9-inch)	**prepared graham cracker crust**
	cinnamon or nutmeg, to garnish

In a 2-quart saucepan, whisk together the eggnog, dry pudding mix, and pumpkin pie spice. Cook over medium heat until very thick and bubbly. Remove from heat and stir in vanilla. Transfer pudding to a bowl and refrigerate until thoroughly chilled.

In a separate bowl, whip heavy cream until peaks form. Beat chilled pudding to soften. Fold in whipped cream until well blended. Spread in crust and sprinkle lightly with cinnamon or nutmeg to garnish. Freeze overnight. Thaw 20–30 minutes before serving. Makes 8 servings.

PEANUT BUTTER CHOCOLATE PIE

I cup	**creamy peanut butter**
³⁄₄ cup	**butter or margarine**
3 cups	**powdered sugar**
2 (9-inch)	**prepared chocolate or graham cracker crusts**
I ³⁄₄ cups	**cold milk**
I small box	**instant chocolate pudding mix**
I container (8 ounces)	**frozen whipped topping,** thawed

In a 3-quart saucepan, heat the peanut butter and butter until butter is completely melted. Slowly stir in powdered sugar until mixture turns into soft dough. Divide and spread mixture evenly over two crusts.

In a 2-quart bowl, beat together the milk and dry pudding mix for I minute. Pour pudding mixture evenly over two pies. Refrigerate for at least I hour. Before serving, spread whipped topping evenly over both pies. Keep leftovers refrigerated. Makes 16 servings.

CREAM CHEESE CHOCOLATE NUT PIE

I container (8 ounces)	**frozen whipped topping,** thawed and divided
I package (8 ounces)	**cream cheese,** softened
I cup	**powdered sugar**
I (10-inch)	**prepared graham cracker crust**
I small box	**instant chocolate pudding mix**
1 ⅓ cups	**milk**
2 to 3 tablespoons	**chopped nuts**

In a small bowl, combine I cup whipped topping, cream cheese, and powdered sugar until smooth. Spread in bottom of crust.

In a separate bowl, beat together the dry pudding mix and milk until smooth. Spread over cream cheese layer. Chill for half an hour. Spread remaining whipped topping over pie. Sprinkle nuts on top. Makes 10 servings.

BANANA CREAM PIE

3 cups	**heavy cream**
¹/₂ cup	**crushed ice**
2 small boxes	**instant banana pudding mix**
1 (9-inch)	**prebaked pie crust**
3	**medium bananas,** sliced and divided
	whipped topping, optional
	sliced almonds, optional

In a 2-quart bowl, beat cream with an electric mixer until it begins to thicken. Add crushed ice. Beat 3–4 minutes more on slow speed. Whip in dry pudding mix at medium speed until blended and mixture becomes stiff. Line bottom and sides of crust with banana slices and then spoon half of the banana cream mixture over bananas. Place another layer of bananas over top. Spoon remaining banana cream mixture over top. Refrigerate for at least 1 hour before serving. Garnish with whipped topping and almonds, if desired. Refrigerate leftovers. Makes 8 servings.

PUMPKIN PUDDING PIE

1 1/4 cups	**cold milk**
1 small box	**instant butterscotch pudding mix**
1 can (15 ounces)	**pumpkin puree**
1 teaspoon	**pumpkin pie spice**
1 (9-inch)	**prepared graham cracker crust whipped cream**

In a 2-quart bowl, whisk together the milk and dry pudding mix for 1–2 minutes. Chill for 5 minutes. Stir in pumpkin and pumpkin pie spice until well blended. Spoon pudding into crust. Refrigerate until ready to serve. Garnish individual servings with a dollop of whipped cream if desired. Makes 8 servings.

CANDY BAR PUDDING PIE

2 regular-sized	**Payday, Baby Ruth, Snickers, or 100 Grand bars,** cut into $1/2$-inch pieces
1 (9-inch)	**prepared chocolate or graham cracker crust**
$1^3/4$ cups	**cold milk**
1 small box	**instant vanilla or chocolate pudding mix**

Sprinkle three-fourths of the candy bar pieces into crust.

In a bowl, whisk together the milk and dry pudding mix until pudding begins to thicken. Spread pudding into pie crust. Refrigerate pie at least 1 hour, or until ready to serve. Sprinkle remaining candy bar pieces over top. Makes 8 servings.

WHITE CHOCOLATE RASPBERRY FREEZER PIE

I cup	**cottage cheese**
³/₄ cup	**cold milk**
¹/₂ cup	**seedless raspberry jam**
I small box	**sugar-free instant white chocolate pudding mix**
I container (8 ounces)	**sugar-free whipped topping**
I (9-inch)	**prepared graham cracker crust**
¹/₂ cup	**raspberries,** optional

In a blender, combine cottage cheese, milk, and jam until smooth. Add dry pudding mix and blend well. Pour pudding mixture into a large bowl and fold in whipped topping. Spoon filling into crust. Cover and freeze for at least 8 hours. Remove from freezer 20–25 minutes before serving. Garnish with fresh raspberries if desired. Makes 8 servings.

NOTE: Sugar-free cheesecake pudding mix can be used in place of white chocolate pudding mix. Sugar-free seedless raspberry jam can also be used if available in your area. Also, regular pudding and whipped topping may be substituted for the sugar-free.

PEACHES AND CREAM PUDDING PIE

1 small box	**instant vanilla or cheesecake pudding mix**
1 1/2 cups	**cold milk**
1 can (15 ounces)	**sliced peaches,** well-drained
1 (9-inch)	**prepared graham cracker crust**
1 1/2 to 2 cups	**frozen whipped topping,** thawed

In a bowl, beat together the dry pudding mix and milk for 1–2 minutes until smooth. Chill until ready to use. Place peaches in crust. Spread pudding over top. Cover and chill for at least 3 hours. Before serving, spread whipped topping evenly over top. Store leftovers in the refrigerator. Makes 8 servings.

EASY EASTER PIE

2 ½ cups	**water**
1 small box	**instant white chocolate pudding mix**
1 small box	**lemon gelatin**
1 container (8 ounces)	**frozen whipped topping,** thawed
1 (9-inch)	**prepared graham cracker crust**

Pour water into a 1½-quart saucepan. Slowly whisk in dry pudding and gelatin mixes over medium-high heat. Bring mixture to a boil, stirring constantly. Boil until mixture begins to thicken and then remove from heat. Refrigerate until thickened and cooled.

Fold whipped topping into cooled mixture and then spoon into crust. Refrigerate for at least 1 hour before serving. Store leftovers in the refrigerator. Makes 8 servings.

VARIATION: Cheesecake pudding mix can be used in place of white chocolate pudding mix. Any berry gelatin can be used in place of lemon gelatin.

CHOCOLATE PEANUT BUTTER LUSH

1 cup	**flour**
2 tablespoons	**sugar**
$^1/_2$ cup	**butter or margarine**
1 cup	**chopped peanuts,** divided
3 $^1/_4$ cups	**cold milk,** divided
2 small boxes	**instant chocolate pudding mix**
$^1/_3$ cup	**creamy peanut butter**
1 container (12 ounces)	**frozen whipped topping,** thawed

Preheat oven to 325 degrees.

In a bowl, combine flour and sugar. Cut butter into flour mixture using a pastry blender. Add $^1/_2$ cup peanuts and continue to work the dough with the pastry blender. Spread into a 9 x 13-inch pan prepared with nonstick spray. Bake for 20–25 minutes; cool completely.

In a medium bowl, beat together 3 cups milk and dry pudding mix for 1–2 minutes. Spread pudding over cooled crust.

In a separate bowl, whisk together the peanut butter and remaining milk until smooth. Whisk in whipped topping until well blended. Gently spread peanut butter mixture over pudding layer. Chill 3–4 hours before serving. Sprinkle remaining peanuts evenly over top. Refrigerate leftovers. Makes 15 servings.

PISTACHIO DREAM SQUARES

1 cup	**chopped pistachios,** divided
1 cup	**flour**
$1/2$ cup	**butter or margarine,** softened
1 package (8 ounces)	**cream cheese**
1 cup	**powdered sugar**
1 container (12 ounces)	**frozen whipped topping,** thawed and divided
4 cups	**cold milk**
2 small boxes	**instant pistachio pudding mix**

Preheat oven to 350 degrees.

In a bowl, combine $1/2$ cup pistachios, flour, and butter until well blended. Press mixture over the bottom of a 9 x 13-inch glass pan prepared with nonstick spray. Bake for 17–20 minutes until golden brown; cool completely.

In a separate bowl, beat together the cream cheese and powdered sugar with an electric mixer until smooth. Fold 1$1/2$ cups whipped topping into cream cheese mixture and then spread over cooled crust.

In another bowl, mix together the milk and dry pudding mix according to package directions. Spoon pudding mixture over cream cheese layer. Chill for at least 1 hour. Just before serving, spread remaining whipped topping over top. Sprinkle remaining pistachios over whipped topping. Store leftovers in the refrigerator. Makes 15 servings.

HEAVENLY COCONUT DELIGHT

1 cup	**flour**
2 tablespoons	**sugar**
1/2 cup	**butter or margarine**
1/2 cup	**chopped cashews or almonds**
1 package (8 ounces)	**cream cheese,** softened
1/4 cup	**sugar**
2 tablespoons	**milk**
1 container (12 ounces)	**frozen whipped topping,** thawed and divided
2 small boxes	**instant coconut cream pudding mix**
3 cups	**milk**
1/2 cup	**coconut,** toasted

Preheat oven to 325 degrees.

In a bowl, combine flour and 2 tablespoons sugar. Cut butter into flour mixture using a pastry blender. Add nuts and continue to work the dough with the pastry blender. Spread mixture in a 9 x 13-inch pan prepared with nonstick spray. Bake for 20–25 minutes. Allow crust to cool completely.

Using an electric mixer, combine cream cheese, 1/4 cup sugar, and 2 tablespoons milk. Fold in 1 cup whipped topping. Spread the cream cheese mixture evenly over the crust.

In a separate bowl, whisk the dry pudding mix into 3 cups milk for about 1 minute, or until pudding begins to thicken. Spread pudding evenly over cream cheese mixture. Cover and refrigerate for 3–4 hours. Before serving, spread remaining whipped topping evenly over the top. Sprinkle toasted coconut over top. Store in refrigerator. Makes 15 servings.

VARIATION: Chocolate, banana, lemon and butterscotch pudding mixes can be substituted for the coconut cream pudding.

BANANA PUDDING SQUARES

1 cup	**flour**
2 tablespoons	**sugar**
¹/₂ cup	**butter or margarine**
¹/₂ cup	**chopped walnuts**
2	**medium bananas,** thinly sliced
2 small boxes	**instant banana pudding mix**
3 cups	**cold milk**
1 container (12 ounces)	**frozen whipped topping,** thawed

Preheat oven to 325 degrees.

In a bowl, combine flour and sugar. Cut butter into flour mixture using a pastry blender. Add nuts and continue to work the dough with the pastry blender. Spread mixture into a 9 x 13-inch pan prepared with nonstick spray. Bake for 20–25 minutes; cool completely.

Place bananas evenly over crust. Whisk together the dry pudding mix and milk for 2 minutes. Spread pudding evenly over banana slices and then chill 3–4 hours. Just before serving, spread whipped topping over top. Store in refrigerator. Makes 15 servings.

CHEESECAKE
PUDDING SQUARES

I box (11 ounces)	**vanilla wafers,** crushed
¹/₂ cup	**butter or margarine,** melted
I package (8 ounces)	**cream cheese,** softened
I cup	**powdered sugar**
I¹/₂ cups	**cold milk**
I small box	**instant cheesecake pudding mix**
I container (8 ounces)	**frozen whipped topping,** thawed
I can (21 ounces)	**cherry, blueberry, or blackberry pie filling**

In a 2-quart bowl, combine the crushed vanilla wafers and melted butter. Pat wafer mixture into the bottom of a 9 x 13-inch glass pan.

In a separate bowl, beat together the cream cheese and powdered sugar. Gradually beat in milk and dry pudding mix until smooth. Chill for 5 minutes in refrigerator. Fold whipped topping into pudding mixture until combined. Spread over cooled crust. Spoon pie filling evenly over top. Chill for at least 2 hours before serving. Store leftovers in refrigerator. Makes 15 servings.

CAKES

APPLE PECAN COFFEE CAKE

4	**eggs**
I cup	**sour cream**
1/2 cup	**vegetable oil**
I	**spice cake mix**
I small box	**instant vanilla pudding mix**
4 to 4 1/2 cups	**peeled and chopped apples**
1/2 cup	**brown sugar**
2 teaspoons	**cinnamon**
1/2 cup	**chopped walnuts**

Preheat oven to 350 degrees.

In a large bowl, beat eggs, sour cream, and oil with an electric mixer until smooth. Beat in cake mix and dry pudding mix and then fold in half of the apples. Spread batter into a 9 x 13-inch pan prepared with nonstick spray. Sprinkle remaining apples over top.

In a small bowl, combine brown sugar, cinnamon, and walnuts and sprinkle over top. Bake for 50–55 minutes. Makes 15 servings.

VARIATION: A powdered sugar glaze can be made by combining powdered sugar, a small amount of water, and a tiny amount of vanilla. Drizzle glaze evenly over the cake to garnish.

BLUEBERRY PUDDING CAKE

1	**white cake mix**
1 can (21 ounces)	**blueberry pie filling**
3	**eggs**
1/2 cup	**sour cream**
1 package (8 ounces)	**cream cheese,** softened
1 small box	**vanilla instant pudding mix**
1 can (16 ounces)	**crushed pineapple,** with juice
1 container (8 ounces)	**frozen whipped topping,** thawed

Preheat oven to 350 degrees.

With a fork, mix together the cake mix, pie filling, and eggs. Gently stir in sour cream. Spread batter into a 9 x 13-inch pan prepared with non-stick spray. Bake 30–35 minutes, or until golden brown. Cool completely.

Mix together the cream cheese, dry pudding mix, and pineapple with juice. Gently fold whipped topping into cream cheese mixture. Spread over cooled cake. Serve immediately or refrigerate. Makes 15 servings.

COOKIES AND CREAM CAKE

1	**white cake mix**
1 ¼ cups	**water**
⅓ cup	**vegetable oil**
3	**egg whites**
1 ½ cups	**crushed Oreo cookies**
1 cup	**cold milk**
1 small box	**instant vanilla or cheesecake pudding mix**
1 teaspoon	**vanilla**
1 container (8 ounces)	**frozen whipped topping,** thawed
5	**Oreo cookies,** broken into small chunks

Preheat oven to 350 degrees.

In a large bowl, combine cake mix, water, oil, and egg whites until smooth. Gently fold in crushed cookies. Spread batter into a 9 x 13-inch pan prepared with nonstick spray. Bake 28–32 minutes, or until a toothpick inserted in the center comes out clean; cool completely.

In a separate bowl, beat together the milk, dry pudding mix, and vanilla until smooth. Fold in whipped topping until well blended. Frost cake and then sprinkle Oreo chunks over top. Serve immediately or refrigerate until ready to serve. Store leftovers in the refrigerator. Makes 15 servings.

ANN'S POPPY SEED CAKE

	sugar
1	**yellow cake mix**
1 small box	**instant vanilla pudding mix**
1 cup	**water**
4	**eggs**
¹/₂ cup	**vegetable oil**
2 tablespoons	**poppy seeds**
1 tablespoon	**almond flavoring**

Preheat oven to 350 degrees.

Prepare a Bundt pan with nonstick spray and then coat with sugar just as you would flour a baking pan.

In a large bowl, combine all ingredients and then pour batter into pan. Lightly sprinkle a little more sugar over batter. Bake for 40–50 minutes, or until golden brown and a toothpick inserted in the center comes out clean. Makes 12–16 servings.

VARIATION: Cake can be baked in two loaf pans for 35–45 minutes, or until golden brown and a toothpick inserted in the center comes out clean.

COCO CABANA
MANDARIN CAKE

1	**yellow or pineapple supreme cake mix**
3	**eggs**
$^1/_2$ cup	**vegetable oil**
$^1/_2$ cup	**applesauce**
1 can (11 ounces)	**mandarin oranges,** drained
1 can (8 ounces)	**crushed pineapple,** with juice
3 tablespoons	**cornstarch**
1 cup	**sugar**
3 to 4	**bananas,** sliced
1 small box	**coconut cream pudding mix**
1 cup	**cold milk**
1 container (8 ounces)	**frozen whipped topping,** thawed
$^1/_3$ cup	**coconut,** toasted

Preheat oven to 350 degrees.

Mix together the cake mix, eggs, oil, and applesauce until smooth. Gently fold in oranges and then pour into a 9 x 13-inch pan prepared with nonstick spray. Bake 30–35 minutes, or until golden brown; let cool.

Prepare glaze by combining pineapple, cornstarch, and sugar in a small saucepan. Cook over medium heat, stirring constantly, until thick and clear. Drizzle evenly over cooled cake.

Just before serving, place bananas on top of glaze. Blend dry pudding mix and milk with a wire whisk and then fold in whipped topping. Spread over cake. Sprinkle coconut over top. Makes 15 servings.

RED VELVET CHOCOLATE CAKE

4	**eggs**
¹/₂ cup	**vegetable oil**
I cup	**water**
I	**red velvet cake mix**
I small box	**instant chocolate pudding mix**
I package (8 ounces)	**cream cheese,** softened
I cup	**cold milk**
I small box	**instant vanilla pudding mix**
I container (8 ounces)	**frozen whipped topping,** thawed

Preheat oven to 350 degrees.

In a large bowl, beat together the eggs, oil, and water. Gradually beat in cake mix and dry chocolate pudding mix until smooth. Pour batter into a 9 x 13-inch pan prepared with nonstick spray. Bake for 35–40 minutes; cool completely.

In a separate bowl, beat together the cream cheese and milk until smooth. Beat in dry vanilla pudding mix. Fold whipped topping into pudding mixture until well blended. Spread topping over cooled cake. Refrigerate before and after serving. Makes 15 servings.

CREAM CHEESE SPICE CAKE

I	**spice cake mix**
$^1/_2$ cup	**pecan gems**
$^3/_4$ cup	**butterscotch chips**
I $^1/_2$ cups	**cold milk**
I package (8 ounces)	**cream cheese,** softened
I small box	**instant cheesecake or coconut cream pudding mix**
I container (8 ounces)	**frozen whipped topping,** thawed

Preheat oven to 350 degrees.

Make cake batter according to package directions. Stir pecan pieces and butterscotch chips into batter. Pour batter into a 9 x 13-inch pan prepared with nonstick spray. Bake 30–35 minutes, or until a tooth-pick inserted in the center comes out clean. Allow cake to cool to room temperature.

In a large bowl, gradually beat milk into cream cheese. Stir in dry pudding mix and then spread over cooled cake. Spread whipped topping over top. Refrigerate until ready to serve. Makes 15 servings.

PUDDING POKE CAKE

1	**white cake mix**
3¾ cups	**cold milk**
2 small boxes	**instant banana pudding mix**

Prepare and bake cake according to package directions for a 9 x 13-inch pan. Remove from oven and immediately poke holes at 1½-inch intervals completely through cake using the round handle of a wooden spoon.

Beat together the milk and dry pudding mix for 1–2 minutes until thick and smooth. Quickly pour half the pudding over warm cake and into the holes. Refrigerate remaining pudding for 10 minutes until set. Spoon over top of cake, swirling to frost. Refrigerate at least 1 hour. Store leftover cake in refrigerator. Makes 15 servings.

VARIATION: For other flavor combinations try using a white cake mix with chocolate, pistachio, coconut cream, or butterscotch pudding; a chocolate cake mix with chocolate, vanilla, cheesecake, or coconut cream pudding; a strawberry cake mix with vanilla or cheesecake pudding; or a spice cake mix with butterscotch, vanilla, or cheesecake pudding.

LEMON YOGURT CAKE

1	**lemon cake mix**
3	**eggs**
1 cup	**water**
$^1/_3$ cup	**vegetable oil**
1 container (8 ounces)	**lemon yogurt**
1 cup	**cold milk**
1 teaspoon	**lemon juice**
1 small box	**instant lemon pudding mix**
1 container (8 ounces)	**frozen whipped topping,** thawed

Preheat oven to 350 degrees.

In a large bowl, beat cake mix, eggs, water, and oil until smooth. Stir yogurt into the batter and then pour into a 9 x 13-inch pan prepared with nonstick spray. Bake for 30–35 minutes, or until golden brown. Completely cool and chill cake for 3 hours or longer.

In a large bowl, beat milk, lemon juice, and dry pudding mix until smooth. Gently fold in whipped topping until thoroughly combined. Spread topping evenly over cake. Serve immediately and store leftovers in the refrigerator. Makes 15 servings.

RASPBERRY YOGURT CAKE

1	**white cake mix**
2 containers (8 ounces each)	**raspberry yogurt with fruit-in-the-bottom,** divided*
1 small box	**instant cheesecake pudding mix**
1½ cups	**cold milk**
1 container (8 ounces)	**frozen whipped topping,** thawed

Preheat oven to 350 degrees.

Mix cake mix with ingredients listed on back of the box. Fold 1 container yogurt into batter. Pour batter into a 9 x 13-inch pan prepared with non-stick spray. Bake for 25–30 minutes until golden brown and starting to crack on top. Using the handle of a wooden spoon, poke holes at 1-inch intervals throughout cake. Allow cake to cool completely.

Whisk together the dry pudding mix and milk for 1 minute until smooth and thick. Spread half of pudding mixture over holes. Refrigerate remaining pudding for 5 minutes. Spread remaining pudding over top. Chill cake for at least 1 hour.

Before serving, fold remaining yogurt into whipped topping. Frost the cake with topping. Refrigerate before and after serving. Makes 15 servings.

*Boysenberry or blueberry yogurt can be substituted.

DEATH-BY-CHOCOLATE CAKE

³/₄ cup	**sour cream**
4	**eggs**
¹/₂ cup	**water**
¹/₂ cup	**vegetable oil**
1	**triple chocolate cake mix**
1 small box	**instant chocolate pudding mix**
³/₄ cup	**semisweet chocolate chips**
2 squares (1 ounce each)	**unsweetened chocolate,** melted and cooled
1 can (14 ounces)	**sweetened condensed milk**
¹/₂ cup	**water**
¹/₂ teaspoon	**vanilla**
1 small box	**instant devil's food pudding mix**
1 cup	**heavy cream**

Preheat oven to 350 degrees.

In a large bowl, beat together the sour cream, eggs, water, and oil until smooth. Gradually beat in cake mix and dry pudding mix. Stir in chocolate chips. Pour batter into a 9 x 13-inch pan prepared with nonstick spray. Bake for 40–45 minutes or until a toothpick inserted in the center comes out clean; cool completely.

Combine melted chocolate and condensed milk. Gradually whisk in water, vanilla, and dry pudding mix until smooth.

In a separate bowl, whip cream until peaks form. Fold whipped cream into chocolate mixture. Spread evenly over cake. Chill 1 hour before serving. Makes 15 servings.

TROPICAL PINEAPPLE CAKE

1	**pineapple supreme, yellow, or white cake mix**
1 package (8 ounces)	**cream cheese,** softened
3	**cups milk,** divided
1 large box	**instant vanilla pudding mix**
1 can (20 ounces)	**pineapple chunks,** drained
1 container (12 ounces)	**frozen whipped topping,** thawed
$^1/_3$ cup	**coconut**

Prepare and bake cake according to package directions for a 9 x 13-inch pan; cool completely.

In a bowl, beat cream cheese with $^1/_2$ cup milk until smooth. Gradually mix in remaining milk and dry pudding mix. Allow pudding to partially set for 5 minutes and then spoon pudding mixture evenly over cake. Sprinkle pineapple chunks over pudding mixture, and then spread whipped topping evenly over top. Sprinkle with coconut and refrigerate until ready to serve. Refrigerate any leftovers. Makes 15 servings.

STRAWBERRY LOVER'S CAKE

1	**strawberry cake mix**
1 large carton (24 ounces)	**frozen sweetened strawberries,** thawed
1 small box	**instant French vanilla, cheesecake, or strawberry crème pudding mix**
2 cups	**milk**
1 container (8 ounces)	**frozen whipped topping,** thawed
	fresh strawberries, sliced

Preheat oven to 350 degrees.

Prepare and bake cake according to package directions for a 9 x 13-inch pan. Allow cake to cool. Cover and refrigerate cake until cold and ready to serve.

Just before serving, poke holes at 1-inch intervals over top of cake using a wooden spoon handle. Spoon strawberries and juice evenly over top of cake, allowing mixture to soak into holes.

In a separate bowl, beat together the dry pudding mix and milk for 1–2 minutes. Chill for 5 minutes to set. Spread pudding over strawberry layer and then spread whipped topping over top. Garnish with sliced strawberries, if desired. Refrigerate any leftovers. Makes 15 servings.

MOM'S MOIST CARROT CAKE

1	**carrot cake mix**
3	**eggs**
1 can (20 ounces)	**crushed pineapple,** with juice
$^1/_2$ cup	**olive oil**
$^3/_4$ cup	**chopped nuts**
1 can (8 ounces)	**crushed pineapple,** with juice
1 small box	**instant coconut cream pudding mix**
1 container (8 ounces)	**frozen whipped topping,** thawed

Preheat oven to 350 degrees.

Beat cake mix, eggs, pineapple, and olive oil together. Stir in nuts.
Pour batter into a 9 x 13-inch pan prepared with nonstick spray. Bake
28–35 minutes, or until a toothpick inserted in the center comes out
clean. Remove cake from oven and let cool 15–20 minutes.

In a bowl, combine pineapple with juice and dry pudding mix. Fold
in whipped topping and then spread over cake. Store any leftovers in
refrigerator. Makes 15 servings.

SUMMER LIME GELATIN CAKE

I	**white cake mix**
I small box	**lime gelatin**
I cup	**boiling water**
$^1/_2$ cup	**cold water**
I small box	**instant cheesecake, vanilla, or lemon pudding mix**
I cup	**cold milk**
I container (8 ounces)	**frozen whipped topping,** thawed

Preheat oven to 350 degrees.

Prepare and bake cake according to package directions for a 9 x 13-inch pan; cool completely.

Poke deep holes into cake with a fork, spacing them about I inch apart. Dissolve gelatin in boiling water. Add cold water to gelatin and slowly pour over cake and into holes. Refrigerate cake while preparing topping.

In a large bowl, whisk together the dry pudding mix and milk until smooth. Fold in whipped topping until well blended. Frost cake immediately and then chill for at least 2 hours before serving. Serve cold and refrigerate any leftovers. Makes 15 servings.

STRAWBERRY CHEESECAKE GELATIN CAKE

I	**white cake mix**
I small box	**strawberry gelatin**
I cup	**boiling water**
$^1/_2$ cup	**cold water**
I small box	**cheesecake pudding mix**
I cup	**milk**
I container (8 ounces)	**frozen whipped topping,** thawed

Preheat oven to 350 degrees.

Make and bake cake according to package directions for a 9 x 13-inch pan; cool completely.

Poke deep holes into cake with a fork, spacing them about I inch apart. Dissolve gelatin in boiling water. Add cold water to gelatin and slowly pour gelatin mixture over cake and into holes. Refrigerate cake while preparing topping.

In a large bowl, whisk together the dry pudding mix and milk until smooth. Fold in whipped topping until well blended. Frost cake immediately and then chill for at least 2 hours before serving. Serve cold and refrigerate any leftovers. Makes 15 servings.

FAMILY FAVORITES

FRUIT DIP

2 containers (8 ounces each)	**plain fat-free yogurt**
1 small box (1 ounce)	**instant sugar-free cheesecake or white chocolate pudding mix**
1 container (8 ounces)	**sugar-free or light frozen whipped topping,** thawed
	fresh fruit, for dipping

In a large bowl, beat together yogurt and dry pudding mix until smooth. Fold in whipped topping until well blended. Serve with fresh fruit for dipping. Makes 12 servings.

NOTE: Regular yogurt, pudding mix, and whipped topping can be substituted.

CREAMY CHOCOLATE PUDDING

1 small box	**instant sugar-free chocolate pudding mix**
1 cup	**cold milk**
2	**cups no sugar added chocolate or vanilla ice cream,** softened*
	whipped topping, optional
	mini chocolate chips, optional

In a large bowl, whisk together the dry pudding mix and milk for 1–2 minutes. Fold in softened ice cream. Chill for at least 1 hour. Garnish with whipped topping and chocolate chips, if desired.

*Cookies and cream ice cream can be substituted.

NOTE: Regular pudding mix and ice cream can be substituted.

STRAWBERRY CREAM PUFF SQUARES

1 cup	**water**
1/2 cup	**butter or margarine**
1 cup	**flour**
4	**eggs**
3 cups	**cold milk,** divided
1 package (8 ounces)	**cream cheese,** softened
2 small boxes	**instant vanilla, cheesecake, or white chocolate pudding mix**
1 container (12 ounces)	**frozen whipped topping,** thawed
	sliced fresh strawberries

Preheat oven to 400 degrees.

In a 2-quart saucepan, bring water and butter to a boil. Stir in flour until mixture forms a ball; remove from heat. Beat in eggs, one at a time, until smooth. Spread dough onto a baking sheet with sides that has been prepared with nonstick spray. Bake 25–28 minutes, or until golden brown; cool completely.

In a large bowl, beat 1/2 cup milk with cream cheese until smooth. Gradually beat in remaining milk and dry pudding mix until smooth. Spread pudding mixture over cooled crust. Spread whipped topping over pudding. Garnish with strawberries. Makes 24–28 squares.

DELECTABLE DIRT PUDDING DESSERT

1	**chocolate cake mix**
1 package (8 ounces)	**cream cheese,** softened
3 1/2 cups	**cold milk,** divided
2 small boxes	**instant chocolate pudding mix**
1 container (8 ounces)	**frozen whipped topping,** thawed
1/2 package	**Oreo cookies,** crushed
	gummy worms, to garnish

Prepare and bake cake according to package directions for a 9 x 13-inch pan. Allow cake to cool completely and then crumble into a large glass bowl or a clean metal pail.

In a separate large bowl, beat cream cheese with 1/2 cup milk until smooth. Gradually add remaining milk and dry pudding mix, blending until thickened. Gently fold whipped topping into the pudding mixture. Spoon pudding mixture evenly over cake crumbs. Sprinkle cookies over top and arrange gummy worms as desired. Refrigerate leftovers. Makes 15–20 servings.

NOTE: Instead of assembling in a bowl, individual servings can be assembled in paper cups by layering cake crumbs, a large spoonful of pudding mixture, cookies, and a gummy worm. Place individual servings on a tray and refrigerate until ready to serve.

EASY CHOCOLATE CAKE

1	**triple chocolate cake mix**
1 small box	**instant devil's food pudding mix**
1 can (12 ounces)	**lemon-lime soda**
1/3 cup	**vegetable oil**
4	**eggs**
1 container (16 ounces)	**chocolate or cream cheese frosting**

Preheat oven to 350 degrees.

In a large bowl, combine cake mix, dry pudding mix, soda, oil, and eggs with an electric mixer. Pour batter into a 9 x 13-inch pan prepared with nonstick spray. Bake 30–35 minutes. Cool and frost. Makes 15 servings.

TRIPLE CHOCOLATE BROWNIES

1 small box	**instant chocolate pudding mix**
2 cups	**milk**
1	**triple chocolate cake mix**
1 3/4 cups	**semisweet chocolate chips**
1 container (16 ounces)	**chocolate frosting**

Preheat oven to 350 degrees.

In a large bowl, whisk together the dry pudding mix and milk according to package directions. Refrigerate for 5 minutes and then stir cake mix into the pudding until blended. Add chocolate chips. Spread batter onto a baking sheet with sides that has been prepared with nonstick spray. Bake for 30–35 minutes. Spread chocolate frosting over top. Makes 24 brownies.

PEANUT CHOCOLATE BUTTERSCOTCH CANDY

I bag (11 ounces)	**butterscotch chips**
2 cups	**semisweet chocolate chips**
I jar (18 ounces)	**creamy peanut butter**
I cup	**butter or margarine**
I small box	**instant vanilla pudding mix**
$2/3$ cup	**milk**
2 pounds	**powdered sugar**
3 cups	**salted peanuts**

In a 3-quart saucepan, combine butterscotch chips, chocolate chips, and creamy peanut butter over medium heat. Stir constantly until chips are completely melted and mixture is smooth. Spread half the mixture over the bottom of a 9 x 13-inch glass pan. Chill in freezer until hard.

Meanwhile, melt butter in a 2-quart saucepan. Add dry pudding mix and milk. Bring to a boil and cook for I minute before removing from heat. Stir powdered sugar into the mixture until well blended. Spread over first layer and then chill in freezer until hardened. Heat the remaining chocolate mixture until melted and then stir in peanuts. Spoon peanut layer evenly over vanilla layer. Freeze for I hour until set. Store in refrigerator before and after serving. Makes 28–32 candy squares.

SIMPLE MOUSSE

1 small box	**instant pudding mix,** any flavor
1½ cups	**milk**
1 container (16 ounces)	**frozen whipped topping,** thawed

In a large bowl, beat together the dry pudding mix and milk for 1–2 minutes. Fold in whipped topping until blended. Refrigerate for at least 1 hour. Serve chilled. Makes 4 servings.

NOTES: If using chocolate pudding, garnish with crushed Oreos or chopped candy bars. If using vanilla, cheesecake, or white chocolate pudding, garnish with raspberries, blueberries, or sliced strawberries. If using banana cream pudding, garnish with sliced bananas.

VANILLA RICE PUDDING

2 small boxes	**instant vanilla pudding mix**
3 1/2 cups	**cold milk**
1/2 container (8 ounces)	**frozen whipped topping,** thawed
1 teaspoon	**vanilla or almond flavoring**
1 cup	**raisins**
2 1/2 cups	**cooked white rice**
	cinnamon

In a large bowl, beat together the dry pudding mix and milk for 2 minutes. Fold in whipped topping. Stir in flavoring, raisins, and rice. Refrigerator until ready to serve. Sprinkle ground cinnamon lightly over top to garnish. Makes 8–10 servings.

NOTE: Sugar-free products can be used in this recipe.

DECADENT BANANA PUDDING

I package (8 ounces)	**cream cheese,** softened
I can (14 ounces)	**sweetened condensed milk**
I large box	**instant banana cream or vanilla pudding mix**
3 cups	**cold milk**
I teaspoon	**vanilla**
$^3/_4$ box (11 ounces)	**vanilla wafers**
4	**bananas,** sliced
I container (8 ounces)	**frozen whipped topping,** thawed

In a large bowl, beat cream cheese and condensed milk using an electric mixer. Beat in dry pudding mix, milk, and vanilla for 1–2 minutes until smooth. Refrigerate for 5 minutes.

Meanwhile, line the bottom and sides of a 9 x 13-inch glass pan with vanilla wafers. Arrange bananas over wafers. Fold half of the whipped topping into pudding mixture and spoon evenly over banana layer. Spread remaining whipped topping over top. Refrigerate until ready to serve. Makes 10–12 servings.

BANANA PUDDING MILK SHAKES

1 ½ cups	**cold milk**
½ small box	**instant banana pudding mix**
1	**medium banana**
5 to 7 scoops	**vanilla ice cream**
	whipped topping

Combine milk, dry pudding mix, and banana together in a blender. Add ice cream, blend until smooth, and top individual servings with a dollop of whipped topping. Makes 6 servings.

VARIATION: Omit the banana from the recipe and try different pudding flavors such as chocolate, vanilla, or strawberry cream.

FROZEN PUODING POPS

1 small box	**instant pudding mix,** any flavor
1/2 cup	**sugar**
3 cups	**cold milk**
14 (3-ounce)	**paper cups**
14	**Popsicle sticks**

In a large bowl, combine dry pudding mix, sugar, and milk. Fill paper cups three-fourths full and then place in the freezer. When starting to set, place Popsicle sticks into the center of each cup. Return to freezer. Serve frozen. Makes 14 pops.

PUDDING-FILLED IDAHO DONUTS

2½ tablespoons	**active dry yeast**
½ cup	**warm water**
1 cup	**unseasoned mashed potatoes**
2 cups	**warm milk**
½ cup	**shortening**
1 cup	**sugar**
3	**eggs**
1½ teaspoons	**salt**
6 cups	**flour**
1 small box	**instant cheesecake, vanilla, or chocolate pudding mix**
2 cups	**cold milk**
	vegetable oil
	cinnamon sugar
	powdered sugar

In a medium bowl, mix together the yeast, water, potatoes, and milk.

In a separate bowl, combine shortening, sugar, eggs, and salt. Stir potato mixture into bowl with egg mixture. Stir in flour 1 cup at a time. Knead dough 1–2 minutes. Cover bowl with plastic wrap and let dough rise 45 minutes or until double in size.

In another bowl, mix together the dry pudding mix and milk until pudding thickens. Place in the refrigerator until ready to fill donuts. Roll out dough to 1-inch thickness on a floured cutting board. Cut dough into 4 x 4-inch squares. Fry dough in hot oil, turning once to make sure it is golden brown on both sides. Dip cooked donuts in cinnamon sugar or powdered sugar and then fill with pudding using a kitchen syringe. Refrigerate any leftovers. Makes 25–30 donuts.

DAZZLING
DESSERTS

BROWNIE PARFAITS

1 box (19.5 ounces)	**brownie mix**
⅔ cup	**chocolate chips**
2 small boxes	**instant white chocolate or chocolate pudding mix**
4 cups	**cold milk**
1 container (16 ounces)	**frozen whipped topping,** thawed
	grated chocolate bar, optional

Prepare brownie batter according to package directions. Stir in chocolate chips. Bake according to package directions for a 9 x 13-inch pan. Allow brownies to cool completely. Crumble cooled brownies into a large bowl.

In a separate bowl, combine dry pudding mix and milk. Chill for 5 minutes. In parfait glasses, layer brownie crumbs, pudding, and whipped topping. Repeat to make three layers. Sprinkle chocolate over each parfait to garnish. Makes 12 large parfaits.

ECLAIR SQUARES

2 small boxes	**instant French vanilla, white chocolate, or cheesecake pudding mix**
3 cups	**milk**
I container (8 ounces)	**frozen whipped topping,** thawed
I box (14 ounces)	**graham crackers**
I container (16 ounces)	**chocolate or cream cheese frosting**

In a large bowl, combine dry pudding mix and milk until smooth. Fold in whipped topping. Cover the bottom of a 9 x 13-inch pan with a layer of whole graham crackers, breaking to fit if necessary. Evenly spread half the pudding mixture over crackers. Place another layer of crackers over pudding mixture. Spread remaining pudding over second graham cracker layer. Top with final layer of graham crackers. Melt chocolate frosting in the microwave 30 seconds. Stir and carefully drizzle frosting over entire surface. Cover and refrigerate a minimum of 3 hours before serving. Makes 15–20 servings.

STRAWBERRY PUFF PASTRY LAYERED DESSERT

1 small box	**instant vanilla or cheesecake pudding mix**
1 1/4 cups	**cold milk**
1 1/2 cups	**frozen whipped topping,** thawed
1 package (17.3 ounces)	**frozen puff pastry,** thawed
3 cups	**sliced strawberries**
	powdered sugar

Preheat oven to 400 degrees.

In a large bowl, beat dry pudding mix and milk until thick and smooth. Fold in whipped topping and chill until ready to use.

Unfold puff pastry and cut along the three folds. Cut each rectangle into 4 equal pieces. Place 2 inches apart on a baking sheet. Bake for 12–15 minutes, or until golden brown. Allow to cool on a wire rack. Divide each pastry into 2 layers creating 48 pastry layers. Set aside 16 good looking tops.

Place 3 to 4 strawberry slices over a pastry square. Using a small teaspoon-sized cookie scoop, drop a dollop of pudding mixture over strawberries and then spread. Top with another pastry square, 3 to 4 more strawberry slices, and another dollop of pudding. Top with one of the reserved tops. Sprinkle powdered sugar over top to garnish. Repeat to assemble the remaining pastry desserts. Makes 16 desserts.

WHITE CHOCOLATE SOFT-SERVE ICE CREAM

1 small box	**instant white chocolate pudding mix**
1 cup	**milk**
2 cups	**vanilla ice cream or frozen yogurt strawberries or raspberries**

In a large bowl, beat dry pudding mix and milk for 1–2 minutes until smooth. Beat in ice cream. Spoon into individual dishes and garnish with berries. Serve immediately. Makes 4–6 servings.

VARIATION: Vanilla, banana, or cheesecake pudding mixes can be used in place of the white chocolate pudding mix.

POUND CAKE TRIFLE

I (16-ounce)	**frozen Sara Lee All Butter Pound Cake,** thawed
I cup	**strawberry or raspberry jam**
2 small boxes	**strawberry or raspberry gelatin**
2 cups	**boiling water**
I cup	**cold water**
I small box	**instant cheesecake or French vanilla pudding mix**
I ¾ cups	**milk**
I container (8 ounces)	**frozen whipped topping,** thawed
	fresh berries, optional

Slice cake into 24 thin slices. Spread jam on one side of 12 cake slices and then cover with another slice of cake, making a sandwich. Arrange cake sandwiches in the bottom of a 9 x 13-inch glass pan.

Dissolve gelatin in boiling water then stir in cold water. Pour liquid evenly over cake sandwiches. Refrigerate for 4 hours or overnight.

In a separate bowl, whisk together the dry pudding mix and milk until thick. Chill for 5 minutes. Spread pudding then whipped topping over set gelatin. Garnish with fresh berries if desired. Makes 16–20 servings.

DRESSED-UP
ANGEL FOOD CAKE

1 small box	**instant cheesecake pudding mix**
2 cups	**cold milk**
1 (9-inch)	**prepared angel food cake**
1 pound	**strawberries,** sliced
1 container (8 ounces)	**frozen whipped topping,** thawed

Make pudding with milk according to package directions. Chill until ready to serve.

Slice cake into 12–14 equal pieces. Place a piece of cake on individual serving plates. Spoon pudding, desired amount of strawberries, and a dollop of whipped cream over cake. Serve immediately. Store any leftovers in refrigerator. Makes 12–14 servings.

NO-BAKE SPRING PUDDING CAKE

1 box (10 count)	**Twinkies,** cut lengthwise in half
1 small box	**instant French vanilla, cheesecake, or white chocolate pudding mix**
1 ½ cups	**milk**
1 can (21 ounces)	**cherry or blueberry pie filling**
1 container (8 ounces)	**frozen whipped topping,** thawed

Form a layer of Twinkie halves cut side up in two long rows of 10 halves each in a 9 x 13-inch glass pan.

In a medium bowl, beat dry pudding mix and milk for 1 minute. Pour pudding mix evenly over Twinkie layer. Spoon pie filling evenly over top and chill for at least 1 hour. Before serving, spread whipped topping over top. Makes 15 servings.

ANGEL FOOD PUDDING PARFAITS

I large box	**instant vanilla pudding mix**
2¾ cups	**cold milk**
I (9-inch)	**angel food cake,** cut into cubes
I bag (16 ounces)	**frozen berry medley,** thawed
I container (8 ounces)	**frozen whipped topping,** thawed

In a bowl, whisk together the dry pudding mix and milk for 1–2 minutes. Chill until ready to use.

In parfait glasses, layer angel food cubes, a scoop of pudding, fruit, and whipped topping. Chill until ready to serve. Makes 10–12 servings.

VARIATION: To make as a trifle, use a glass bowl and layer half of the cake cubes, half of the pudding, and a third of the berries. Repeat layers. Top with whipped topping and remaining berries. Makes 10–12 servings.

BLUEBERRY PUNCH BOWL CAKE

1	**white cake mix**
2 small boxes	**instant cheesecake or vanilla pudding mix**
4 cups	**milk**
1 can (20 ounces)	**crushed pineapple,** drained
1 can (21 ounces)	**blueberry pie filling**
1 container (12 ounces)	**frozen whipped topping,** thawed
1/2 cup	**chopped nuts**

Prepare and bake cake according to package directions for a 9 x 13-inch pan prepared with nonstick spray; cool completely.

In a bowl, beat together the dry pudding mix and milk until smooth. Chill until ready to use.

Cut cooled cake into bite-size squares. Place half of the cake cubes in the bottom of a punch bowl. Spoon half of the pudding over cake. Spoon pineapple evenly over pudding layer and place the remaining cake squares over pineapple. Spoon remaining pudding over cake and spread pie filling over pudding. Top with whipped topping and sprinkle with nuts. Refrigerate before and after serving. Makes 16 servings.

FALL TRIFLE

1 box (19.5 ounces)	**brownie mix**
1 small box	**instant chocolate pudding mix**
1/2 cup	**water**
1 can (14 ounces)	**sweetened condensed milk**
1 container (8 ounces)	**frozen whipped topping,** thawed
1 bag (8 ounces)	**toffee bits,** divided
1 container (12 ounces)	**frozen whipped topping,** thawed

Prepare and bake brownies according to package directions for a
9 x 13-inch pan; cool completely. Once cooled, cut brownies into
bite-size squares.

In a large bowl, beat dry pudding mix, water, and condensed milk until
well blended. Fold the 8-ounce whipped topping into pudding mixture.

In a large glass bowl, layer half the brownie squares, one-third of the
toffee bits, half the pudding mixture, and half of the 12-ounce whipped
topping. Repeat layers. Sprinkle remaining toffee bits over top. Refrigerate for 3–4 hours before serving. Store any leftovers in the refrigerator.
Makes 16 servings.

CHERRY CHEESECAKE TRIFLE

1 small box	**sugar-free cherry gelatin**
1 cup	**boiling water**
1 (9-inch)	**angel food cake,** cut into cubes
1 can (20 ounces)	**reduced-sugar cherry pie filling**
1 cup	**cold milk**
1 small box	**instant cheesecake pudding mix**
1 container (8 ounces)	**fat-free frozen whipped topping,** thawed

In a small bowl, combine gelatin and boiling water until gelatin is completely dissolved. Chill for 20 minutes.

Place half the angel food cubes in bottom of a large trifle or glass bowl. Drizzle half the gelatin mixture over top. Spoon half the pie filling over soaked cubes and then repeat layers.

In a separate bowl, combine milk and dry pudding mix until thick and smooth. Fold in whipped topping until thoroughly combined. Spread over layers in bowl. Refrigerate for 2–4 hours before serving. Store leftovers in refrigerator. Makes 16 servings.

NOTE: Regular gelatin, pie filling, and whipped topping can be substituted.

PUMPKIN SPICE TRIFLE

1 cup	**pumpkin puree**
1/2 cup	**water**
1/2 cup	**applesauce**
3	**eggs**
1	**spice cake mix**
3 small boxes	**instant vanilla or cheesecake pudding mix**
2 1/2 cups	**cold milk**
1 container (8 ounces)	**frozen whipped topping,** thawed
1 cup	**chopped pecans**
1 cup	**English toffee bits**

Preheat oven to 350 degrees.

In a large bowl, beat pumpkin puree, water, applesauce, and eggs until smooth. Gradually stir in cake mix and 1 box dry pudding mix. Spread batter into a 9 x 13-inch pan prepared with nonstick spray. Bake for 40–45 minutes. Allow cake to cool completely.

In a separate bowl, beat remaining dry pudding mix and milk together for 1–2 minutes until smooth. Chill for 5 minutes. Fold whipped topping into pudding until well blended.

Crumble one-third of the cake in the bottom of a large glass bowl. Spoon one-third of the pudding topping evenly over cake layer. Sprinkle with one-third of the pecans and one-third of the toffee bits. Repeat all layers two more times. Refrigerate before and after serving. Makes 16 servings.

COOKIES AND CREAM BROWNIE TRIFLE

1 box (19.5 ounces)	**brownie mix**
2 small boxes	**instant white chocolate or vanilla pudding mix**
3⅔ cups	**cold milk**
1 package (1 pound, 1 ounce)	**Oreo cookies,** chopped
1 container (12 ounces)	**frozen whipped topping,** thawed

Make and bake brownies according to package directions for a 9 x 13-inch pan. Allow brownies to cool and then crumble or cut into bite-size pieces. Stir together the dry pudding mix and milk for 1–2 minutes. Chill for 5 minutes.

In a glass punch bowl, layer half the brownie crumbs, half the pudding, and one-third of the cookies. Repeat layers. Spread whipped topping over top. Sprinkle remaining cookies over top. Serve immediately. Refrigerate any leftovers. Makes 16 servings.

PEANUT BUTTER CUP PIZZA

I bag (17.5 ounces)	**peanut butter or sugar cookie mix**
I small box	**instant vanilla or chocolate pudding mix**
I ½ cups	**cold milk**
½ cup	**plain yogurt**
⅓ cup	**peanut butter**
I ½ cups	**chopped peanut butter cup candies**

Preheat oven to 350 degrees.

Make the cookie dough according to package directions and spread thinly to cover a baking sheet that has been prepared with nonstick spray. Bake 10–14 minutes, or until lightly golden brown around edges. Allow crust to cool completely.

Beat together the dry pudding mix, milk, yogurt, and peanut butter until smooth. Chill for 10 minutes. Before serving, spread pudding mixture over crust. Sprinkle chopped candy over top. Makes 20 servings.

CHOCOLATE CHIP COOKIE PIZZA

1 roll (16.5 ounces)	**refrigerated chocolate chip cookie dough**
1 ½ cups	**cold milk**
1 small box	**instant chocolate pudding mix**
½ cup	**plain yogurt**
⅓ cup	**creamy peanut butter**
	sliced bananas, shredded coconut, chocolate chips, miniature marshmallows, or chopped candy bars

Preheat oven to 350 degrees.

Spread dough thinly to cover a 12-inch pizza pan. Bake 10–12 minutes, or until golden brown. Allow to cool completely.

In a separate bowl, combine milk, dry pudding mix, yogurt, and peanut butter until smooth and thick. Chill 5–10 minutes, or until pudding mixture sets; spread over crust. Sprinkle toppings of choice over pizza. Refrigerate before and after serving. Makes 12 servings.

ANGEL FOOD COCONUT PUDDING ROLL

I can (20 ounces)	**crushed pineapple,** drained
2 teaspoons	**coconut flavoring,** divided
I box (16 ounces)	**angel food cake mix**
I small box	**instant coconut cream or vanilla pudding mix**
I cup	**cold milk**
I container (8 ounces)	**frozen whipped topping,** thawed **powdered sugar**

Preheat oven to 350 degrees.

In a large bowl, combine pineapple and 1½ teaspoons coconut flavoring. Stir in angel food cake mix until well blended. Line an 11 x 17-inch baking sheet with sides with parchment paper. Spread cake batter on pan. Bake for 18–24 minutes, or until golden and springs back when touched. Remove from pan with parchment paper still attached and place on a wire rack. Allow cake to cool completely.

Beat together the dry pudding mix, remaining flavoring, and milk for 1–2 minutes until smooth. Chill for 5–10 minutes in refrigerator. Fold whipped topping into pudding until thoroughly combined. Refrigerate until ready to use.

Spread pudding mixture over cake. Begin rolling the cake starting on one short side, carefully removing the parchment paper from the bottom as you roll. Lay rolled cake seam-side down on a serving platter. Chill until ready to serve. Sprinkle powdered sugar over top to garnish. Slice to serve. Makes 10 servings.

NOTES

NOTES

NOTES

NOTES

NOTES

METRIC CONVERSION CHART

Volume Measurements		Weight Measurements		Temperature Conversion	
U.S.	Metric	U.S.	Metric	Fahrenheit	Celsius
1 teaspoon	5 ml	1/2 ounce	15 g	250	120
1 tablespoon	15 ml	1 ounce	30 g	300	150
1/4 cup	60 ml	3 ounces	90 g	325	160
1/3 cup	75 ml	4 ounces	115 g	350	180
1/2 cup	125 ml	8 ounces	225 g	375	190
2/3 cup	150 ml	12 ounces	350 g	400	200
3/4 cup	175 ml	1 pound	450 g	425	220
1 cup	250 ml	2 1/4 pounds	1 kg	450	230

 Check out these "101" favorites
for more tasty recipes:

Cake Mix	**Slow Cooker**
More Cake Mix	**More Slow Cooker**
Chocolate	**BBQ**
Gelatin	**Casserole**
Yogurt	**Dutch Oven**
Mac & Cheese	**Toaster Oven**
Ramen Noodles	**Chicken**
Salad	**Rotisserie Chicken**
Zucchini	**Ground Beef**
Tofu	**Meatballs**
Tortilla	**Grits**
Canned Biscuits	**Potato**
Canned Soup	

Each 128 pages, $9.99

Available at bookstores or directly
from GIBBS SMITH
1.800.835.4993
www.gibbs-smith.com

ABOUT THE AUTHOR

Stephanie Ashcraft, author of the original *101 Things To Do With A Cake Mix*, has taught cooking classes based on the tips and meals in her cookbooks for almost ten years. She lives in Tucson, Arizona, with her husband and four children. Stephanie, a native of Kirklin, Indiana, graduated from Brigham Young University with a degree in family science. This is her 14th cookbook.